I0815395

THE KWANZAA STORY

Celebrating Culture through Community

Alliah L. Agostini
Illustrated by Olivia Smith H.

becker&mayer! kids

The story of Kwanzaa began during a time when Black people in America had enough of not having enough. They knew they deserved equal access to more. To better.

Better schools.

Better jobs.

Better housing.

And on a steamy August night in 1965, the people of Watts, a mostly Black neighborhood in Los Angeles, California, knew they deserved better treatment from the local police.

This time, they rebelled. They fought back for an entire week.

This would become known as the Watts Rebellion. By the end, many people were hurt, buildings were destroyed, and the entire community was in pain. Everyone needed to rebuild and heal.

But our story didn't start with struggle. Our ancestors lived throughout the African continent, a land the size of three Americas. It was the home of tiny villages and great kingdoms, many different groups and traditions, and over 1,000 languages. But Africa would be forever changed by losing many of its greatest treasures: most importantly, its people.

For years, European enslavers forced millions of African people to work for no pay in faraway places, colonies like the land that would become America. Enslaved Africans tried to hold on to the culture of their homeland, but memories faded with each generation born on American soil.

American slavery lasted for hundreds of years, but enslaved people and their allies fought for freedom until slavery was outlawed after the Civil War in 1865.

Life after slavery was still very difficult, but some newly freed people became educators, business owners, and even government leaders. However, others saw their growing power as a threat, and Black people's freedom was again limited by laws that treated people differently because of the color of their skin.

The Watts Rebellion wasn't the first time our people fought back, and it wouldn't be the last. Black people across America were tired of being treated like their lives didn't matter and decided to use their voices and their actions to create lasting change. New generations of activists (people who work hard to bring about change) pressed on into the 1900s. They were motivated to help Black people achieve equality.

Important leaders like Ida B. Wells-Barnett and W. E. B. Du Bois and organizations like the National Association for the Advancement of Colored People (NAACP) organized to bring unfair experiences to light and fight for equal rights, while activists like Marcus Garvey encouraged Black people worldwide to be proud of their African heritage and to create their own businesses and communities.

Starting in the 1950s, the Civil Rights Movement included leaders like Reverend Dr. Martin Luther King Jr., who fought for Black Americans' equal rights with large nonviolent protests, and Nation of Islam leader Malcolm X, who encouraged people to have pride in their Black heritage through his powerful speeches that encouraged fighting inequality by any means necessary.

Because of these new ideas, the Civil Rights Movement grew into the Black Power Movement. Named for activist Stokely Carmichael's chant, "Black Power!", it encouraged Black people to love themselves, unite, and heal their communities. In 1966, California college students Huey Newton and Bobby Seale started the Black Panther Party, a group that supported Black people with health programs and education about their rights.

In Los Angeles a year earlier, an activist and teacher named Ron Everett started a group called **US**. Ron wanted to make things better for Black people after the Watts Rebellion. **US** started as an African culture and history study group whose members believed Black Power and healing should come through a cultural revolution, living a life inspired by Africa, their ancestors' homeland.

To show that they were true in their beliefs, Ron and other members learned how to speak Swahili, Africa's most widely spoken language, and adopted Swahili names. Ron changed his name to Maulana Karenga, meaning "Master Teacher." Mothers ran the School of Afro-American Culture for the children, teaching **US**'s beliefs and Swahili. To celebrate their culture, the **US** members wore afros or shaved heads, African-inspired clothing, and dark sunglasses. They even created their own African-inspired celebrations for weddings and funerals.

US members no longer celebrated the holidays they used to, so some of their children were disappointed. They wondered what they could celebrate instead. Maulana Karenga and other **US** members researched African holiday traditions that could inspire the group's own holiday. They found harvest celebrations like South Africa's Natal/Zululand seven-day Umkhosi celebration. Umkhosi took place at the end of the year and celebrated ancestors and community leadership. It involved festive song and dance, feasting, and a taste of the first crops of the year.

The new holiday would be cultural, not religious, and run from December 26 through January 1. It would happen after Christmas so even people who were not members of **US** could celebrate too. Historically, this also had been one of the few times during the year when enslaved people were given time off to rest.

This new holiday would be a chance for people to celebrate their culture and community, reflect on the past year, and reset for the year ahead. The holiday would be called Kwanza, from the Swahili word meaning "first fruits"—*matunda* ("fruits") and *ya kwanza* ("first").

US lived by *Kawaida* (Swahili for "as usually done"), a list of 161 principles or main ideas focused on living an African-inspired life in America. Publicly they only shared the Nguzo Saba, seven of these principles. They decided Kwanza would follow these principles too, one being celebrated on each of the holiday's seven days.

The first principle was named **UMOJA**, or unity—to establish a sense of togetherness in our families, communities, nation, and the African diaspora, or the many places where African-descended people live around the world.

The second principle, **KUJICHAGULIA**, was self-determination—our individual ability to define, name, create, and speak for ourselves.

The third principle, **UJIMA**, focused on collective work and responsibility—to work together to build and maintain our community.

The fourth principle, **UJAMAA**, stood for cooperative economics—a commitment to make and support Black businesses.

The fifth principle, **NIA**, meant purpose—to make everyone's focus the building of the community to restore Black people to their original greatness.

The sixth principle, **KUUMBA**, was creativity—to make our communities more beautiful and fruitful than they were when we arrived.

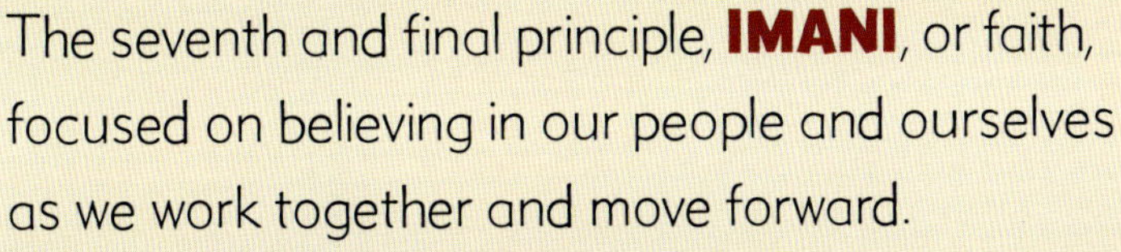

The seventh and final principle, **IMANI**, or faith, focused on believing in our people and ourselves as we work together and move forward.

US also selected seven symbols to use in their celebrations. The first was the *kinara*, or candle holder. It represented African ancestors and Black freedom fighters. The kinara holds seven *mishumaa*, or candles—three red candles on the left, representing the struggle; a black candle in the center, for people of African descent; and three green candles on the right, representing the environment and a hopeful future. Each candle also symbolizes one of the seven principles.

A *mkeka*, or straw mat, placed in front of the kinara would be covered by *muhindi*, or ears of corn. Each ear represented a child in the household, or one was placed to represent the children in the community. A *mazao*, a basket of fruit, represented the harvest. The *kikombe cha umoja*, or unity cup, was a shared cup to be passed during the nightly candle ceremony while acknowledging ancestors who had passed on.

During each night's ceremony, the phrase "Habari Gani!?" meaning "What's the news?" would be declared along with the day's principle, ideally by participating children. The kikombe cha umoja would be raised by an elder in tribute to the ancestors, as attendees shout "Harambee!" meaning "Let's unite!" seven times.

One candle would be lit each night, starting with the black candle in the middle of the kinara (Umoja). On the second night, the red candle on its left would be lit (Kujichagulia), and on the third night, the green candle to its right (Ujima). The lighting pattern would continue—red (Ujamaa), green (Nia), red (Kuumba), green (Imani)—until the final night.

A *karamu*, a large community feast, would be held on December 31. The seventh symbol, Zawadi, or thoughtful, handmade gifts, were to be given out to children on the last day of celebration, January 1.

The first day of the new holiday was held at the *Hekalu* (Swahili for "temple"), the **US** headquarters, on December 26, 1966. Maulana held a contest to encourage members to decorate their homes in red, black, and green, Marcus Garvey's symbolic colors of African liberation.

After celebrating in their homes through the week, **US** members and nonmembers assembled for the first karamu on December 31. Everyone sat on floor pillows, wore beautiful African clothing, brought symbolic food to share, and drummed in celebration. Ngao Damu led the ceremony, encouraging attendees to look back on the year and reflect on what they did for the Black community.

The children also participated, acting out stories about African royalty. For one performance, six children were each given a letter to spell out "Kwanza," but a seventh child wanted to participate, so a second "A" was added, turning Kwanz**a** into Kwanz**aa**.

Starting in the late 1960s, excitement around the Kwanzaa holiday spread as Black people across America were drawn to this new way to celebrate their heritage.

Kwanzaa started to be celebrated by other **US** chapters and in cities where the Black Power Movement was strong, like San Diego's **US** chapter in 1967. Oakland, California, and other nearby states soon followed thanks to Harriet Smith (also known as Sister Makinya), a student leader whom Maulana encouraged to spread the holiday.

Across the country in Newark, New Jersey, activist and poet Amiri Baraka became an advocate for **US** and Kwanzaa. In 1970, Amiri shared the idea of Kwanzaa with attendees of the African Congress, a Black leadership unity conference he organized in Atlanta. In New York City, Kwanzaa was being celebrated in boroughs from Brooklyn to Manhattan. Harlem children were taught about Kwanzaa by a teenage pastor named Alfred "Al" Sharpton. In Chicago and Philadelphia, individual community organizations started their own observances until they came together to form larger citywide celebrations.

Black community organizations, schools, religious groups, and media around the country kept learning about Kwanzaa and brought it to life in their own communities.

Some newer celebrators leaned on the Nguzo Saba as their lives changed in the 1980s. Because of activists' efforts, Black people now had more access to jobs, education, and even neighborhoods that were once out of reach. But some felt alone in their new communities. To find togetherness, some people joined organizations like Kwanzaa Clubs and a Black family organization called Jack & Jill, which encouraged Kwanzaa celebrations to reconnect with members' African heritage.

Kwanzaa may have started with US, but its growth was now powered by Black people across America.

In the 1990s, there was a new moment of Black pride with hip-hop music, fashion, and movies, including a very important one about Malcolm X's life starring Denzel Washington. Kwanzaa became more mainstream. It was now celebrated in public schools, large museums, churches, and even at fancy celebrity parties. Big companies also caught on and made Kwanzaa-themed advertisements, decorations, and cards, and they sponsored Kwanzaa events to reach Black customers.

The United States government even started to acknowledge the holiday, starting in 1993 with President Bill Clinton's first Kwanzaa presidential proclamation, and again in 1997, with a special postage stamp created by artist Synthia Saint James.

Still a young holiday, Kwanzaa is now celebrated by tens of millions of people in communities across America and beyond. Each celebration is similar but has its own flair, from small ceremonies at home to joyous community ceremonies and festivals with performers, storytellers, musicians, and dancers of all ages.

Today, interest in Kwanzaa is growing as once-young celebrators start to adopt the tradition for their own families to celebrate their pride in their Black culture. For those who celebrate, Kwanzaa is a collective cultural recharge, an annual reset as we look back to refocus as we move forward.

Though the holiday has shifted from its homegrown roots into a well-known annual tradition, it's important to remember Kwanzaa's main purpose—to celebrate your history, your heritage, your community, and yourself!

Kwanzaa was created by US, for us, and continues to be powered by us all.

BLACK AMERICAN CULTURAL HOLIDAYS

Did you know Kwanzaa isn't the only holiday Black Americans created to have deeper ties to Black culture? Others include Black Love Day (February 13, before Valentine's Day), Umoja Karamu (the fourth Sunday in November, an alternative Thanksgiving), and Juneteenth (June 19th and, to some, "Black Independence Day"), now a federal holiday celebrating when the last enslaved Americans were freed. While February's Black History Month is well known, most people have not heard of Black August, which celebrates Black freedom fighters and historical August events like the March on Washington and the Watts Rebellion. Like Kwanzaa, each holiday was started by someone who wanted to give us another way to celebrate and have pride in our history and culture.

TIMELINE

3000 BC The Egyptian kingdom rules as the earliest known kingdom in Africa. It would become the first of many.

1500s–1800s The transatlantic slave trade starts, bringing West Africans to colonies around the world.

1526 Spain attempts to establish the first slave colony in current-day America. It fails after enslaved people fight back.

1619 Angolans kidnapped by English enslavers land in the Jamestown colony, now Virginia. This is the official start of American slavery.

April 9, 1865 The Civil War ends, signaling the end of slavery in the United States along with the Thirteenth Amendment.

February 12, 1909 W. E. B. Du Bois and Ida B. Wells-Barnett are among the founders of the NAACP, an organization fighting for the rights of Black Americans.

July 20, 1914 Marcus Garvey founds the UNIA to inspire Black unity and pride for African descendants around the world.

1954–1968 The Civil Rights Movement, a massive effort to end racial segregation, is led by notable leaders such as Dr. Martin Luther King Jr. and Malcolm X.

August 11–16, 1965 Black residents of the Los Angeles Watts neighborhood fight back against unequal rights and unfair treatment for almost a week.

Mid-1960s–early 1970s The Black Power Movement encourages Black pride, unity, and justice.

September 7, 1965 **US**, a Black Power group motivated to live life inspired by Black unity and love for the culture, is founded by Dr. Maulana Karenga.

December 1965 Children of **US** members ask about creating a new holiday to celebrate Black culture.

October 15, 1966 The Black Panther Party is founded by Huey Newton and Bobby Seale to help empower Black people with social services.

December 26, 1966 Inspired by research on African harvest traditions and **US**'s Kawaida principles, **US** holds the first Kwanza in Los Angeles, California.

December 31, 1966 Kwanz**a** becomes Kwanz**aa** at the first karamu.

Late 1960s Kwanzaa spreads—first to San Diego, then to northern California, and then to other centers of the Black Power movement across the United States.

September 4–7, 1970 Amiri Baraka shares Kwanzaa with Black leaders attending the Congress of African People in Atlanta.

1980s–1990s Along with an increase of Black pride in movies, music, and fashion, Kwanzaa becomes popular and is celebrated across schools, churches, and organizations.

1993 Bill Clinton is the first United States president to recognize Kwanzaa with a presidential proclamation.

1997 The United States Postal Service issues the first Kwanzaa stamp.

2008 Barack Obama is elected the first Black United States president.

2018 The Marvel movie *Black Panther*, about a regal superhero from the mythical African nation Wakanda, becomes a global phenomenon and sparks interest in science fiction and fantasy themes that celebrate Black history and culture.

2020 The Black Lives Matter movement renews Black America's continued fight for equal rights and sense of pride.

2021 Celebrated in Texas since 1865, Juneteenth becomes an American federal holiday.

2025 Kwanzaa marks its sixtieth year as a holiday.

MY KWANZAA CONNECTION

Kwanzaa has been an informal part of my holiday season since the late '80s/early '90s when I was about eight or nine years old. While our family didn't celebrate daily, we always attended community Kwanzaa celebrations in my hometown of Buffalo, New York. Buffalo had celebrated Kwanzaa since at least the mid-1970s; Dr. Maulana Karenga, now the chair of the African American studies department at Cal State, would even speak at Kwanzaa events in Buffalo nearly every year. I happily remember celebrations at community institutions like the Langston Hughes Center, my grandparents' home, and even the holiday parties of Jack & Jill, an organization I was in as a child and am now in with my own family. I also think of our community storytellers, Sharon Holley and Karima Amin, who, among others, were stewards of our local Kwanzaa tradition.

A couple of years ago, my daughter asked why we didn't celebrate Kwanzaa at home, though we attended community celebrations in New Jersey, where we now live. (Children's questions make great inspiration!) The reason was an honest one—holiday burnout! But we finally celebrated Kwanzaa for the very first time at home in 2024, and I am so glad we did. It wasn't exhausting. It was the recharge we needed.

Our first night was shared by four generations, with my then-ninety-three-year-old grandfather as our presiding elder. Each night was powerful. As our daughter recited the daily principles, we reflected on their meanings and took turns honoring our family's ancestors whose lives reminded us of each principle.

Kwanzaa is not without its critics, and its origins are not without some controversy. Big changes in our world have not historically happened easily, and the state of the Black Power Movement when Kwanzaa was born is certainly no exception.

People also have tried to dismiss Kwanzaa as "playing African" or a "made up" holiday simply because it comes from the recent past. But Kwanzaa was created to help African Americans plug into an important culture stolen from them while dealing with the persistent, ever-changing struggles of a complicated new homeland.

But at its core, the holiday was born from a need to help restore Black people's sense of self, even though there was constant injustice—injustice that would sadly not end after the holiday's founding. The principles of Kwanzaa and the reasons to celebrate are just as important now as they were in 1966. We live in a time where some of the many rights our elders and ancestors fought for are in danger of falling apart.

Whether you celebrate is your choice—but it's never too late to start! For many Black parents, myself included, raising our children to have belief in themselves, our past, and our heritage is one of the most important things we can do. Celebrating Kwanzaa is one of many ways to do this. It is an empowering way to focus on our culture, our history, and ourselves so we can enter each year with intention.

What's your Kwanzaa connection, and how will you celebrate?

To the Young-Fergs.
The spirit of Ujima lives in you all.

First published in 2025 by becker&mayer!kids, an imprint of The Quarto Group,
142 West 36th Street, 4th Floor, New York, NY 10018, USA
(212) 779-4972 www.Quarto.com

EEA Representation, WTS Tax d.o.o.,
Žanova ulica 3, 4000 Kranj, Slovenia.
www.wts-tax.si

10 9 8 7 6 5 4 3 2 1

ISBN: 978-0-7603-9932-3

Digital edition published in 2025
eISBN: 978-0-7603-9933-0

Library of Congress Control Number: 2025933886

Group Publisher: Rage Kindelsperger
Creative Director: Laura Drew
Managing Editor: Cara Donaldson
Art Director: Scott Richardson
Cover and Interior Design: Scott Richardson

Printed in Huizhou, Guangdong, China TT062025

Editor's Note: In the late 1960s, Stokely Carmichael moved to Africa and soon after adopted the name Kwame Ture. We refer to him as Stokely here as that was his chosen name when he famously led a crowd of supporters in the inspiring "Black Power!" chant.

Lexile® 1250L